Our Photographs

JON GLOVER

Our Photographs

Published in 1986 by
CARCANET PRESS LIMITED
208–212 Corn Exchange, Manchester M4 3BQ, UK
and 108 East 31st Street, New York, NY 10016, USA

British Library Cataloguing in Publication Data
Glover, Jon
  Our photographs
  I. Title
  821'.914 PR6057.L63

ISBN 0–85635–649–2

The publisher acknowledges the financial assistance of the Arts
Council of Great Britain.

Typeset by Dentset, Oxford
Printed in England by SRP Ltd, Exeter

For Elaine
Abigail and Rhiannon

Acknowledgements
Some of these poems have been published in
Poetry and Audience (Leeds), *Stand* and *PN
Review*. Thanks are due to the editors of these
journals. Several groups from the sequence have
been read on 'Poetry Now' (BBC Radio 3) in
programmes introduced by Jon Silkin and
Michael Schmidt. Seventeen appeared as a
Northern House Pamphlet, *The Wall and the
Candle*, Newcastle-on-Tyne, 1982

Contents

This sequence of poems concerns a man who leaves his home on a Scottish island for the United States in the nineteenth century. It also concerns the place he sets out from and the people who stay behind. His sense of space and of himself changes. His letters home disturb those who remain to face eviction. Who has gone away?

Making Ready

It was as though they fell willingly into place.
Behind barred doors and darkened windows
they sat tending evening fires. A few pulled
half-grown vegetables and carried heavy sacks
to secret shelter. After going about their
business in the hopeless private evening
they set themselves to rest in unconscious reward.
The night was cloudy and there was no moon.
Sleep was easy and expected.

I saw a garden where new weeds thickened
entwining and shading each worthless, forced
luxury. By the end of summer they were everywhere.
Then the first gales tore them down and they
matted themselves over the thin unusable crops.
Grass pricked out its slow return. And all around
the people stood unmoved and still. The place was
awaiting completion. They were so utterly
unimportant they were rooted to the spot.

To Quit

"... and leave for your own good."

So I did not wait for any bailiff or agent. I wanted not even
to admit that much of his dispossession. To fight for this
land would put me like a speck of dust on that clean
accountant's finger. In whatever Capital he wrote his
assurances, I saw with what infinite care he might blow
away that small encumbrance. Either he held the land, or
me. Such ownership lightly edged me off his charts. I
crossed from shore to shore. Then by boat to Oban and
then to Dundee. Waiting to embark, I sat and watched the
evening mist lick out under the sunshine, softening into
the steely mudflats of the Tay. On a tiny rectangle of
wood, a man painted a picture of the shore with its farms
and fat cattle as though it was a desolate and storm-swept
beach. Obliterating the marks of men, his landscape
brushed out my love, family, blood. Deep in the ship to
Boston I woke to the slap and rush of the water at my ear.
The painter's grey, heartless waves followed through
every night.

Two Passengers

Looking out to sea, standing
on deck by the Captain's cabin,
you are firm but at ease.
A regular passenger.

Face immobile, but I feel
you relish this time-
tabled space between
responsible worlds.

Your landscapes! Your flowers!
Taking always the wider view
you blink in the sun, relaxing,
composing the worth of it all.

Meanwhile, the ferry steams
and shudders by the quayside.
My four hundredth crossing
this year; even so, I must

examine the chart each time
and check every gauge. At
four this morning I inspected
the coal yards. Monday:

the Company's crew are
obedient and neat,
fresh from Church
(and the benefits of

Sunday's adult education
classes). We welcome
the passengers with
loyal respect. Despite

our skills in navigation and
engineering they know their
place. I only record one poor
soul removing from the island

today. He will be kept out of
sight until the others have left
the ship. Below decks, for the first
time he smells the machinery of state.

Conversation Piece

The Captain had one heavy leather suitcase
that stayed permanently on the ship:
a collection that he added to less and
less frequently now that his voyages
were never (intentionally) more than
forty miles each way. Only at the
half-way point between the two quays
(thirty more minutes) would he sometimes
open the case, having locked his door
and given strict instructions to the
First Officer. Occasionally, he would
choose one object to stand on the table
when a respected client of the Company
was invited to his cabin to pass the time
over an appropriate drink. Today, thinking
of the rich passenger still standing at
the rail, he opened the case and chose
a dried, curled armadillo (from Florida),
a Chinese opium pipe, (his Uncle's)
sketch pad from the Nile delta and
a glass-topped box containing five
mounted scorpions. The ship heeled in a
tide race. He shifted his balance, glanced
at the sky, replaced three of the objects
in the case and slid it under his bunk.
He arranged glasses and a decanter and
opened the door. He spoke to the passenger
who entered briskly, accustomed to being
noticed. They sat opposite each other
at the brass-edged table. Land soon filled
the porthole's view. Five minutes remained
to repossess the savage outer world
in polite, deliberate conversation.

V
The Artist's Grim Humour

"Recorded it." Not the grass of cattle,
but His. The landscape achieved
for the classics — legend and nobility —
but not for bright Italian saints.
Such coloured morality seems cheap
beside what I know of His wrath.
I have enough to contend with.

I study what etchings come from London.
The copying will teach me though it spoils my eyes.
Their vision, the masters', must have been gifted.
I've not that, it seems, but I'm not content
with my style. Accuracy I can work on.
And when I paint it in with colours
the masters might use I have some escape
from the Church and the muck of my neighbour's farm.
The moving sea parades what anger I can allow.
Secretly, with my finest nib, I might copy
their human figures. Style, style will come,
may come. For now, this formal, public storm
will do. Scrub out the blobbed people. Varnish it.

The Painter and Science

My paintings assemble in one bright room
their gloomy imprecisions
and accumulate their insults and accusations
leaving so much untouched, unnamed.
Next to the pile I keep an old sextant;
my grandfather was a sea captain.
Its brass is still polished and each
moving lens and filter holds some dignity
in its smooth passage. Tantalizing
and strangely coloured, its sense of place
is immaculate. What might science know!
The sun reflected and turned through
there and there, fixed in metal rings
and green glass; the horizon numbered
by the finest engraving. I know the
thing lies complete, though I cannot use it,
and still I regard guiltily its way
of seeing. In its smooth, teak box
it seems content with the world's spinning
while my poised waves and sunless, unexplored
pastures are mere imagination, simply human.

VII
On the Ship: Memories

Above the village, the walled graves.
To go up to that ceremony,
climbing into silence,
was no division. That mile stamped
a god's dream over the land.
Our hill held in each stone mark
the words we left between peat and root.

"Worship the house with its boned roof.
Worship the tree with its seasonal berries.
Worship the water, fingering from the hillside.
Stay, stay in every step of grass.
The wind blows sand out of the sea
into this land."

We once saw another ship pass miles away.
And though there was no way to speak
we all watched it move. Our new freedom
ached without words. I searched the sea
for whales, porpoises, any living thing
that would say the whole sea was not mine.
But there was nothing to know.
The ship held us like a cage,
and salt cracked our skin
till we were disgusted with love.

Islanders

I want to begin that I don't know
how to speak to you.
But that's not true. I have
to say where I am — see:
a salt spring, a creek, a sandy forest.
The water is bitter
and lies in a burned-out log.
I followed an Indian path here
from where I was thrown off the railroad.
I could see the farmsteads. I've learned
not to go there. Children watch
me though, and all the others.
The young see us travelling; their parents
forget such journeys. I go on
to these meeting places and
here are men from the Isles.
And from the islands of Sweden,
Iceland, Finland, fishermen too.
I trap gulls for them.
And why should I stop like these farmers?
Through the trees, I saw a lake
that seemed endless. That's enough.
I don't want their English names.
As they turn their backs on the passing trains
I seem to hurt them, and, perhaps,
they still hurt me. As I drink,
an Indian looks at me and through me
straight at the earth. He was born
near the spring, he says, and he touches
the water for me. I can go now.
You understand this, don't you?
He will take this letter for you all
to some village here. He touches the trees
for each word: Westmannaeyjar, Rauma,
Calgary, Oland. I don't want
to hear the English, or to know their names.

Pure

I picked handfuls of fruit. At the edge of the fields, shaded by sumac and maple, English apples and cherries dropped, thin and sticky, into the brown stubble. No trace of whatever farmstead had once been here with its precious, sweet fruit; the seeds, carried from some old, careful orchard; saplings guarded in this heat and the dispiriting ice. A new field edges into the forest here, and the trees, too, uproot the first paths, fences and corner posts. But deeper, by the creek, the Indian's well stands in its log.

> And again I peered into the log.
> The water was smoothed by the
> wood's fiery colours: copper
> and salt sifted their warmth
> through the clouds' reflections.
> The new world, its freshness,
> its spiked, dangerous brilliance,
> softened into a depth
> I dared not measure.
>
> Deft mosses, elegant spiders
> spangled each nearby tree.
> But not the smooth well.
> Alone and silent, away
> from the wasps, it marked
> its own territory; its human
> purposes a permanence of sorts.
> Pure? Or pure indifference?
> I can't see my face in it.

Away

Pool of water, pool of water. I have thrown three stones now and you tell me nothing. I want some voice, some speech from this place. But my stones fall in the dull weed and will not match my anger. The letter comes from the other place and talks of endless forests and the long wait by the railroad tracks. Where is he? I have come to the shore perhaps to see where that world might be. In the village they watch me. I am now in the outside. Rocks, rocks, are these the same sounds he hears? He writes much of the heat, his gun, the moving bands of people. No place for birth, marriage, death. Nowhere that is the outside, the far. He travels day by day and yet seems to possess it all. I have left the village with his letter. Outside by the rock pools I am outside, in silence, and I possess nothing.

Natural Speech

A sour contempt completes that rough dialogue.
Equipped simply by frowns and disbelief
departure drags out along the severe cart track
which rises far over the village and then jerks
and stumbles down to a lake with its edge of
reeds and lazy flies. A river flows in beside the
track that I followed and leaves again behind
a distant mountain shoulder. No houses, boats or
livestock. Owners and tenants live on the other
sides of this hidden bowl. Yet their absence
alarms my footsteps. Alone in the high air
silent pressures of wings disturb this captivating
freedom. Streams preserve their covert voices.
The grass twitches its messages to the morning
sun. This alluring, natural escape I fear, propelled
into rhetoric, the disowned British language.

The Deserted Lake

In the reeds a model ship, perhaps three feet long,
rested (its work done for the day?). Yet the whole
place was deserted. What strange child, or man,
would have brought it here and then forgotten it?
Or, confident that it would never be found,
have left it, tied up, ready for tomorrow's voyage?

It had four masts and spars with sails furled and
neat rigging. There was also a funnel; obviously
a sophisticated view of the future: the best
energies of two worlds. No local fishing boat
but a liner ready for deep waters. It was new.
The deck planking had not darkened in the sun,

the varnish was clear and each tiny brass block
and screw was shining. It was protected from
the lake's few ripples by an enormous, black-
based grass clump. I stooped towards the water
to wash my face. The ship's reflection shivered
and parted. I slipped, splashed mud all over the

deck and tipped the ship on its beam ends.
It rocked briefly among the bubbles and angry
larvae, its harbour sadly altered, the grass
trampled and muddy. Having precipitated this
playful earthquake in someone's solitary kingdom
I emptied my shoes and resumed my steady course.

Harvest

Split from the rock,
their yellows and blacks smear to green;
the mussels' soft shine lies bruising in the sun.
Such stillness seems not to have needed life.

Yet they patch together their sharp, stitched colony
against whatever element frets the stone.
Each clasps a portion of the sea that aches
over it, lapping its primitive fresh gape.

For a time there is flesh: liquid, defiant,
unhurt even by the stupid, tiny pearls
that crush out to dust,
without sound, in the sand.

Their shape is savage,
bound to the rock,
small, black, sacred books
opening and closing for their own commemoration.

Over the machair, I see those incessant, pulling mouths,
twenty sheep still on the eyebright and thyme.

The Dream

Fear? The morning wind ruffled into my sleep.
Through one eye I saw a praying mantis
jerk to stillness on my arm. God! the cold
sunshine made the thing flame against the sky.
When the last of my breath had left me
I jumped from shelter casting the harmless insect
away and I dared not look at my arm
till the air grew hot and I stopped to rest.
On my skin that spring of life and death
shivered all day. When I closed my eyes
I remembered the dream: I stood beside a
child's small grave in a sandy forest.
In the dream I slept nearby when the
mourners were gone. And, waking then,
the insect's light feet pinned death in
my limbs and I had to kick out and run from it.
I ask you now, who has died?

The Last Sermon

The rest of you. We have not left,
and cannot leave. I speak of your duty
and here I give you its image.

You know your slaughtered animals,
the heads' features slit to shadow.
You remember the blood, without pulse
but falling from the white fat's edge.

Would you drain life away, end allegiance,
as you stop life in your cattle?
The blood of your thoughts is here in your birthplace,
held as your skulls hold your simple souls.

Listen. When I studied, my friend was a doctor.
On his table were spread slivers of flesh to plot
in the microscope; colours like maps of the new world.
I stared through his lens in wonder but I saw no life.

Would you be like these fragments?
Leave, and your bodies will scatter
on the Churchless ground, stilled and soulless
as those butchered, empty heads.

Letters and Fictions

One in America, the rest now scattered
or dying here by the shore, the recovery of love
seems beyond any task permitted by hunger and cold.
God knows, I believed no one could just go.
The world was not to be trifled with.
I was a tenant and obedient to the will of the place.
Though still I thought my love crossed enough boundaries.
And now his journeys consume my present,
and his past is freed, cancelled rather,
by each new marvel. He describes flowers in such
    profusion
I think he is mad. Paradise? It wasn't promised
for the price of a voyage. The sea and the land are work,
work and death, and as for love
all I want is to finish it and sleep.

"I saw enormous lilies. They were red and gold.
The summer sun is so bright I could not believe
nature could go on matching it, radiance for radiance.
Orchards, wheat-fields and the rich, cracking mud.
The smell of heat. Who needs to praise God
amongst this opulence? I met a painter who simply
records what is there: orchids, poison ivy and
the humming-birds no Northerner has seen.
This observation, again and again, is love.
My senses grow, and desire."

Now the village is burnt, his letters will have no answer.
They become fictions.

Words and Miracles

Without thinking, I took this book from the Church. As I passed at dusk the door blew open in invitation, I thought, though it cried the place's emptiness. Stealing silent words, wrath neglected my act. His powers seemed cashed elsewhere. Now, sitting in my shelter by the rocks, I could tear its pages from indifference. Its love ceased by the shore. The New World our only miracle, and that known to be too far for most. The old people, struck still and quiet by the effort of each measuring breath, come and read from it. Names, successions, rewards, families: but silence grows in them. Winter squeezes miracles out of their blood. Promises, kingdoms, possessions fade with the body's heat.

A doctor, visiting to investigate conditions took the book with other interesting things. Now they can die in peace.

Abandoned

Those children sleep in the bracken.
Could I see such close, cool greenness?
All that lacy, drifting stuff the clouds glow through —
it befriends my memory. Yet the words for it
spin about into nothing clear. Bracken, grass;
if I recall its lush, stiff, white liquor,
its uncurling touch, I still have nothing
of those desperate beds, their place of cold awakening,
gagged death. The grass is here and here.
Where I stretch my hand it seems too warm to fix
into that unflinching mat that wraps each failing breath.
What I touch gives me lies?

Nature

I stop for hours to watch butterflies. I am tempted not to
draw them but to collect them. Sometimes I think I would
like to watch them grow and breed. Then I fancy
arranging them, to kill and preserve their abundance,
their colours, their alien delicacy. Still I have nowhere for
this. And, finally, to set things in a house would create a
stillness shut from the sun, a civilization that I go on
trying to leave.

> From earth colours and its skin
> of thin, dry crystal,
> its fragile liquids snap out and are gone.
> Without tenderness
> or anything sensual
> it holds my gaze, meets food,
> flower or parasite
> across void after void:
> the blank spaces come
> and go on coming.
>
> Touching their fine dusts
> tempts me to indifference —
> all those designs, fantastic eyes,
> and mimicked leaves grow
> without fear or knowledge,
> display purpose and beauty
> without love and die raggedly
> or freeze. These human qualities
> want them collected, row upon row,
> preserving each as a separate
> kingdom of man's desire?
> Like cold, pinned galaxies?

Treasures

The faint smell of a distant, injured skunk
announced the evening's parley. The sky cleared
from orange to green to blue to perfect
black, thrilling with stars. Horizons faded.

I was alone with the closed, ravenous
freedoms where bats swung their zany forage
trails through the trees in the rich air that was
still and dry and sweet. Insects' noisy, rattling

talk, the small animals' feverish hunt
and owls' insistent, proud flight settled in
their routines. Sightless yearnings apportioned
night's energies, consumed day's peaceful

heat. Sitting beside the road, I heard a
desperate scuffling in a nearby ditch.
When it had stopped, I felt in my pocket
for the brilliant monarch wings and goldfinch

feathers picked from the roadside's coarse litter
that morning and lovingly wrapped in clean
paper. I dropped them into the reeds. When
I woke, at dawn, a contorted, blinded

snake lay by the ditch. It discounted all
innocent concern as its lurid blood
dried; dismal treasure, night's discovery.
Unsure, daylight cajoled its gritty wound.

XXI
Portraits and Love

Remembering, trying to love, I write about standing by the shore, I want your face, not fixed as in a portrait but moving. And automatically you turn away. Why should this come so naturally, to make you go back over the sand? Trees, the valley, herons flap slowly over the bay. Gone. The picture smirks in the sun: the past unloved, its imagined objects dispossessed.

> The sand pushes its colours
> into the sun: streaks of silver,
> lavender spines of seaweed,
> green and rock-black wood, the drift
> and smell of the sea and all
> that the other continents spit.
> There are close-nailed crates,
> their bright fruit wrung out;
> nets; rust; a tube of ointment
> labelled in Russian script;
> and pumice, floating cargo
> of a battered ship: stone flung
> and floated absurdly, suds
> of the earth's heat,
> on to this cooler shore.

So nothing: waste, nicely composed. Your anger is there, without question and I don't care.

Last Letters, Last Photograph

It rained. My pockets filled. Papers, letters
clumped and stiffened. They weighed more
than their words seemed fit for. Autumn rain,
not to be avoided; the written leaves
had reached their season. I felt

for the sodden, gluey mementoes;
pressed and picked at the travelling inks.
Hates, expectations and pleas
tore across each other and parted: a curdle
of blue fibres. Soundlessly, the breeze

tugged out your meanings. That other world
softened its old resolve; its estates disclosed;
vows unspeakable. In the centre, one photograph,
used to the wet, survived. Later, it dried, then
curled by the fire like the blotted surface of a map.

The continents rolled to the east, a land on edge.
The sea, ash-grey, hung like a cliff. All the roads
doubled back. The roofs peeled. I could see you
walking on windows. Bodies slipped to the grass.
Gravity defied, that punishing scene tipped
clear into the past. I could only look back.

The Wall and the Candle

The stone wall (ridiculous to speak
of its loved creation) weighs out
a hillside field. Community of man
and frost-split rock? moss and insect?

So much rough work; and the bracken will rise
each summer to hide it, rain slides
through it: such warnings are some
recompense. Boundaries marked naturally

but to order, and thus instructive,
they apportion life or landscape
as you will. In composed degradation
the tame and the wild meet at this

closed corner: earth floor, turf
and the one wall which runs back
for miles, blackly counting its
larger property. And the light

permits less and less of the world
to serve our winter. My candle flaps
its huddled ceremony of power over
beasts; drips away. Spray, frost, dew,

and the first shoots of the walled crops
glitter nearby. But hypnotically,
in the dark, the tallow trickles and clouds
to a cluster of smoky jewels

as the flame, someone's commodity,
reaches the end of what is paid for.
The night and the wall insist we have just
such molten value in your rich imagination.

Boundaries

Spreading, the light sifts and drums
into undetailed silver. It tips the sea
to the horizon. Only the thunder,
cracking overhead, ruffles its liquid
pressures that way. Watching, following,
from cloud to cloud, over the water,
it spills into the inhuman distance.
A story? Refused, the mirror creases
under the wind, and rain pricks quick
waves like grass in the floods. Not
that way. Such pictures can't be true.

XXV
Waiting

A skin outgrown, transparently broken
from love, casts to the unfelt places.

For an easy human death such raw abrasions
prepare their accounts. So much desire.

Pulse, unpersuaded, thins like the hanging rain:
uncentred, ageless, prepared for nothing.

Seen from a Distance

The sea is glassy today. Appropriately, a well-polished steam launch brings the tropical garden expert to rig out the most sheltered hillside in flowers of the uncultivated world. Botany for pleasure (and proof that the climate isn't so bad). And, indeed, we must be up to date, experimental even, in retirement.

Directing the erasure of the native wood the gardener plans a complex wilderness. Sitting beside his case of neatly labelled seeds he displays prints of Indian hill-stations and African jungle. Later, in the house, the owner tours his water-colours of Scottish castles deep in New England forest and Malayan plantations. Eucalyptus and palm, gathered in such savage places, take quickly and bring the Empire together.

> From the cliff-top the sea's
> drift and grain spreads perfectly
> beneath the hot, rising air.
> Quickly trying the sun, its
> black, slithering communities
> circle, stiffen and vanish
> under the brittle light.
> Over on the shadowed side
> of the bay one fisherman,
> darkly clothed, lets his boat
> drift and leans nearer and
> nearer the bleak surface.
> Slowly, the wash of a steamer
> bends the whole thing.
> The boat slops upright.
> Light settles again,
> allowing nothing to be seen.

Owning Seaweed

Ends of mild water,
only soft to this touch.
To the waves, the frost,
the brushed rock they are
printless and unimpressed.
Brown, many-lobed lights
they glint, wash and vanish
like ripe bud walls in the sea.

Unpeel, bulge, glass over.
It is not there: perfect.
Nothing wants this. It is
made too clearly.

The table is set. Precisions,
edges: a desperate order
consuming hunger. This water
sluiced from the thunder,
the sky's crackling unease.
Drink.

"Compared to [Staffa] what are the cathedrals or the palaces built by men!"

Sir Joseph Banks, James Cook's naturalist, 1772

The Last Funeral: Maps and Images

A long tide hunked the rolling, abraded flesh
up the sand. Cornered and shredded in its
devoted rock pool its translucent pall
trickled away to the low, Spring surf. Briefly
to be discovered; an odd gesture of creation;
a stammer on the landscape's tongue,
ah! demanding the distinct language of Nature.

Six hours distant clamour and the sea
dutifully replaced its simple map over the bay.
The rock pool and its contents were erased;
the matter withdrawn, unsightly and unsited.
A tide race, beyond the point, proffered its own
careful solution; the true contours softly
dismembered; breathless, shining liquids;

incomparable, another record to be unspoken. And so,
as though wonderfully invisible, their cathedrals –

Remembering the History Book

The Romans: clear line drawings on stiff, glazed paper.
A neat river curves in imperturbable perspective
beside a spaced and fearless wood. A horizon, gentle
hills; the sky's intense blue conveyed by parallel lines
ruled in a clever expansion. Three birds, the sun, two
   clouds.
Four slaves tend the gardens, tie up a boat, bring wine
to the mistress who sits politely beside a mosaic
in the centre of her villa. (The mosaic is preserved,
we are told, though its colours are disappointing.
Better in the line drawing? Well, more quickly passed
   over.)
There is a detail: a snake, a bird singing, two dogs
strain from the patterned edge towards a delicate
   fountain.
Its clarity, its divided loyalties are there to walk on.

> Your breath, your heart-beat
> is laid out in stone. The quick
> feathers, the weight of your
> eyes: a colonial arrangement.
> Progressive, civilized,
> its persistence relishes
> the living. Consuming songs
> flatly hymn the dangerous
> master. Wonders, aqueducts,
> columns of words, prescribed
> cruelties; these, our foundations.
> Our eloquent wars engrave our
> possessions. Industry thrives.

Another History Book

Sixteenth century engravings
review the conduct of the native
inhabitants. Imagine the artist
beginning his official duty
with the quickly sketched first
sight of the coastline, first
forest, first Indians. Then
the brutal rites and wars.
Here, the classical mode is
strongest. His humanistic
training matures as he attends
to the bodies carefully dismembered for burning and scalps
held over a fire for smoky
preservation. Torture, medicine,
retribution learned from which
gods? Shaking and sick in his
cabin he unwraps his precious
paper and prepares a fitting
record. It is all clarified,
(but did he see that?) as
he sweats out his vision of
perfect proportion. The Italian
anatomists will not free his
eyes. The more he sickens and
the more he disbelieves the
greater his technical assurance.
His explorations bravely continue
with turtles, snakes and alligators.
On returning to London
he finds that he has dropped
completely out of fashion.

New Maps: Exchanging Gifts

Passing the boundaries of the early maps,
the partitions of major rivers, coastlines,
hills and lakes we continue a conquest,
in outline, at least. A picture story
of what has been walked across and seen.
The remaining possibilities are disproportionately
small (on paper). Far into the interior, by the
high falls, comes a point of exchange. The price
of further discoveries is high: all that historic
vision, truth for truth. But the unmarked land
demands its revelation. Accounts must be rendered.
Each gives the other the articulate sense of where
he is. The passing of gifts begins a new record
which settles its view like ink on a printer's
stone. It will be reproduced and sold.

Roman Arena

Noticing the frilled, purple flowers,
the sheen of undisturbed, powdery attraction;
noticing the arched, painless margins
of reds and blues and flesh-streaked white;
noticing the weightless ellipses;
the prickling, sun-blinded crowns of pollen;
the traps, tongues and heartless floods

the Renaissance brimmed in his eyes;
his drawing faltered and he ran to
the stockade fence, pressed his hands
on the barbed logs and stared (loving,
shocked and silent). Before the trees
was a stone arena its high doorways
black and steady despite the shimmering

air. Such an achievement! The blocks
of stone so large they looked as though
their perfect geometries measured
a gigantic, unworked pain into the earth.
He remembered the unreliable maps.
Where were his people? A cry from the
centre of this upturned quarry echoed

naturally through the forest. Birds fluttered.
He threw his pen at the high summer light.

Revenge

Summer's imperial creatures spit and scum the grass forks,
their dark, uncurious blades. A wet net of bubbles
cools a grub. Such a fine, bloodless womb survives
the sun. It is enough for this time. Other pods
rattle their beauties to the wind. Hollow stalks,

crisp fruits, creamy chambers preen to perfection.
Fleeting, safe possession. Unmarked bells chime
their ceremonies, announce their new ones.
Their deaths and illnesses go unrevealed because
they must. In the unclaimed spaces the eye crafts

luckless values but their memories slip. Too near,
the lens-closed light sparkles. Minute geometries
double their power. The last walls accord with
their horizons. Past the ferns, past the trees,
the exquisite grass illuminates some sky.

Whose ripples? Whose waves? Summer clouds compose
their letters of exclusion. A gunshot achieves the lie
of the land. Echoes love the walls. My shoulder aches.

Riches for the Birds

Another elaborate funeral. Memories,
homage, the protestation that this
life was unexpectedly valuable. Guards
arrange their special roles, space
their power, enclose the easing dead.

Which slips away behind the armory
of intent regret. Scabbed and corroded
it runs its stifled course, relieves
the moments of routine and
attracts a quick fear as it passes.

Like a circle of birds which
prey for a second and disperse into
devouring isolation. The pretty animals
have yielded. Stabbed fish, torn eye,
peeled voice. These trophies lift away
and settle for the night. Justice,
seen to be done, bides its time.

Hiding Again

This energy soon outrun
I cannot look at the ground.
Resting and staring upwards
the trees seem clear enough
and then the sky. Waiting
through daylight for the
cold night the brilliant
wind draws my sweat.
I do not move. The
silence of the pine forest
concludes the search.
It settles like a neatly
coiled rope at the
beginning of a voyage.

He must be brought to account for this act. A disturbed mind. Hardened, no doubt, by years of unrewarding toil. There shall be no place for anyone who takes life. The hunt for the murderer will concentrate the values of those who knew the victim. It will be remembered. We will be grateful to have been reminded. An outcast. There can be no return.

The forest casts adrift.
Rocks slip quietly aside.
Needles bed their journey.
The timber recedes:
hull-down on the horizon.
Through the foam,
the sleeping gulls,
steering by the stars
the spaces open for
as far as my body needs.
The spars do not creak,
there is no spray.
The canvas presses
towards any new world.
Another escape from justice?

Wasted Talent

And now, painting the town, I seem to have
still more choice views. I set up my easel
in a field from where I can see the whole
thing: after the wheat and poppies
the first houses, mills and chimneys,
spaces where roads and rivers flow,
the railway's cutting towards the
domed town hall. Bricks and slate
deliver blocks of mass, weighty colours,
after the modern fashion. On the road
to my left a farmer walks into town,
three mill workers walk to their
cottages. They pass beside an elm
and a dusty barn. Putting in all that
detail gives movement and a hidden
story. So what is this town
(a piled, squared-off echo of
tall clouds) surrounded by flowers,
hedges and my representative figures?

I set up again in a lane behind a high mill.
My stool and easel scrape on the cobbles
as I shift to look closer at the moss,
the sky reflected in a large puddle,
the weeds enlivening a disused chimney pot.

I painted one brick, bright and wet as a
ruby sea-anemone, its perspective
studiously correct. A triumph.

Time Out

Taking a journey to the West Coast I left industry behind
and sat expectantly in the train for a first sight of a new
sea, its highly reputed light and its Romantic islands. And
there . . . At a halt before the last descent to the coast I
jumped down and pulled my luggage and painting things
out too. Leaving the cases with a signalman I walked past
the platform to the edge of a steep incline. I started work
immediately. The coast curved in towards a placid
harbour sheltered by small, low islands, and in the
distance, slightly misty, but luminous and expectant, the
first Hebridean mountains. A backcloth of theatrical
splendour! A clue, a dream, a temptation!

> But how to confine the stone,
> quayside warehouses? The stacked
> fish crates? Arranged on the
> pier for their necessary journeys
> oil drums, tea chests and fire
> wood, and, between the end
> of the railway line and the
> steam-ship berth the rounded
> stocks of coal. These natural
> resources, graded and respected
> concluded this holiday composition;
> a landscape not quite good
> enough: unmarketable again.

Our Photographs

"If cows clatter to the iron-stained stream.
If the weight of a stone displays man's work.
If the summer's hot mud puffs up into a mist of flies."

Remember our qualities recorded
in proper fabrics that weave
through the photographic paper.
We were still, attentive,
and watched the eyes, fears,
the other people's looks of how it was
that light out here in salt and silver.
Portraits: a thorough chemical process,
like visiting the lawyer for a deed,
a will, confirming ownership.

This, a house, and a road going west.
Trees around the edge are not there
part of the meaning. It's a road
that goes somewhere and that's important.
But light smudges over the windows
and the horizon is black despite the sun.
All that's left is what you don't want
to see. The picture won't care for you.
What we composed and framed, beyond death,
is your worthless trash, like history.

The Antique Shop

Pillowed, sickly surfaces;
established fabrics; covetous
gloss; brass-edged, approved
memories; the scored, wooden
weights of age; the limpid
scars of work, of prized
utility, of love aching in
the shiny dark (family ties
iridescent in a newly silvered
mirror). Breathless, the blank
spots crowd the Victorian
looking-glasses which top
the soft drawers of miniatures,
unlocked cases of gold and jet,
dull, crimped lockets:
the catches' pretty betrayal —
final, unloved objects of love,
cloudy, unreflective and public.
Each practised hinge swings
wide the disproved values, loosing
the unnamed faces of the dead, briefly
fingered by the future auctioneers.

Meal Times

Musical clock: symphonies of bird-song, built
"with the best materials and up to date factory
methods". Reeds and pipes twitter their marvels
across the polished table, surprise the upholstery,
open all doors. Inside its case, the wood is razored
clean. Outside, pictured, aged with a penknife,
it pronounces a wild authenticity. Methodical
springs untwist into sound that glitters between
the knives and hisses in the glasses (each
with its bulging, reflected window frames.
Catching the sun!) Wound, observed and dusted,
it times the maple sugar, the gales, the silver's
tarnish. It allows for work with a natural note.
Such democratic joy outclasses the old continent.

Commercial Art

Although, in this painting, the North Sea
is a true, whistling grey; although the clouds
race with unsettling clarity; although
the measured, spiky whitecaps crease and spray
the chosen breadth of water as far
as the eye can see this clipper tips the waves
with inexcusable weightlessness (at an angle
as bravely jaunty as that struck by the pre-
Muybridge race-horse in the next canvas
whose two front legs reach forward and
back legs trail, as though trapped,
while it prices up the aristocratic turf).

The artist has added a few spots of colour
(triumphant sunshine between the worst,
most bulbous clouds, for example, and a
bright ensign and pennant) which assure
the Line's trim future, running before
the wind, confident of the Trades. And,
a nice detail, the Master's dog stands
to attention (though the likely crates of
chickens and harassed sheep seem invisible)
beside the wheel, singled for the Company's
honour even if implausibly balanced.
Passing by this lucky rigging we see

'Hazy Cornfield', 'Lakeside Pebbles', 'Two
Children in a Tree', 'The (forgotten) Shoe'.
Neatly glazed, commerce, adventure and
moving landscapes outrun their times.
The walls invite decoration but the occasions
just escape, outgrowing their trophies,
nudging from behind the entrancing scrap.

National Parks

Railway tracks relay our colonies. Bands of men
briefly outlive their civilization spiking an
iron grid of further wealth. A bright dream maps
on to the figured rocks, lumber and ore. And
quickly re-routed, the station waiting-room
finds use as the village library. Connections
fall back, the past re-assembles, the old
pictures open and close.

> Uncoloured autumn plants; yet
> they stain the pitched, loose track.
> Strong stems curl and press,
> re-marking their softer energies.
> A last growth of Europe's seeds
> strips through the country.
> If there is nothing left
> but this dull, tendrilled ribbon?

The land has been felt. It won't stir itself to
any more meaning. You can't join me.

Microscopes and Flora

A common garden? The species of summer
machair to be reviewed: the exciting
distances of common land; of the lens's
bloodless, circular Doomsday; free domain
of science. Preferred exploration records,
names and drafts the miniature partitions
of class and order as the objective glass
blooms over justly refracted information.

Prized as a land unpeopled and unaccounted,
blown into life and belaboured into
such rich study, the bay settles under
its new witnesses. At the end of the day
new forms of botanical community
have advanced over the paper. Roots and
lively dependencies emerge. Through the
late, floating June light each table multiplies.

During the short Northern nights details like
these seem silently commended by every
known star. The darkness is sure. And then, each
morning, the extraordinary high
tides of sun prepare the open banks of
common flowers; daisies, bird's foot trefoil,
cranesbill, the glossy points of saxifrage,
and all the uncoveted, fertile scents.

And if these numbered cells become my beauties
truly to be loved as lists of knowledge
in notebooks filled with the orchids' tender
illumination and by brush and pencil
neatly licked into shape? What would this passion
miss, solidly worked, day by day, from the

water lines to the most elevated rocks?
Dunes, marram, machair, grass, wet-land, alpines:
natural history warms to its task,
its instruments clarify unrealised lineage
private glory struck so near and yet so far,
estrangement magnified into rarity.

The Landlord's Northern Summer

The holly tree shines
and flickers its pale,
summer leaves. A flock
of sparrows dares its
cool, unreliable caves
for the season's grubs
and tumbles out into
the brittle light.
Then tries the crude,
tattered roses that
thud on the window,
careening the new stems
that bend, scratch and
grieve against the wall
to press home their
flowering. The wet ground
unseals its final larvae,
and drifts of midges
curdle the sudden air.
Swifts bestride these
clouds of proven luxury.

The landlord, alarmed, sealed this document, queried two words in the Dictionary and was certain, after consulting the Field Guide, that one of the sparrows was a goldfinch. Then, while boiling water for his coffee, he refined the memory of a lizard that he had seen slowly traversing a warm house wall just below the eaves late, one holiday night in the South. There it was, lazily gripping the cracked plaster, curving radiantly over the surplus heat. Certain, he toppled a forest, cleared the lakeside and, firmly, in the beds of shale, plotted a power station.

Defining the Past

The afternoon was hot and misty. The lake was flat
and yellow. Thirty children and a teacher walked
in silence to the end of the road and then scrambled
down the steep bank to the narrow shoreline.
High clouds bloomed in the mist. The light became
greyer. The children gathered round the teacher
as he stood proudly against the bank: a lesson
in geology. They looked down at the slatey rock on
which they stood and noted the angle at which it
sloped into the water, split by parallel fissures
and decaying into powdery shingle. Above that, the
edge of brown, sandy soil, six feet of glacial
wash-out, old rivers and silty floods. Here, an inch
of dark red grit: imagine that clearly coloured
layer rolling off for miles three feet under farms
and forests. The sky was divided now by a hard edge,
the taunting sunlight's frill narrowed as green
and purple shreds brushed the tree tops. At the top
of the bank a few inches of dark loam plumed with
grass and silver, oozing roots: nature's latest
achievement. But the children were no longer looking
at the strata of the place's million year history.
The lightning cracked and they ran, broke into
thunderous freedom, the torrents drumming in their
    heads.
They kicked and slithered up the bank, across a field
and towards a wood. Dangerously splashing from tree to
tree and sucking the water that ran down their faces
they pushed through a hedge on to a farm track and
reached a barn where they sheltered beside calm horses.
They crouched breathlessly on the dusty floor.
The teacher caught up with them and turned their escape
to good account. The barn's construction and timbers
were of great historical interest. For tomorrow
he planned an interesting lesson on static electricity.

Evening in the Museum

Filtered sunshine sweetens the glass,
hollows the shades of velvety display
and picks out the day's new dust.

In the evolutionary sequence,
this polished room honours the suave,
tongueless shells —

the uncashable, spell-binding
legacies of which ancestors?
And then the curtained, air-

proof cases of Victorian exotic
moths, ranked in odourless, worthy
burial. Is it so important

that the life has gone? Classified,
interchangeable conquests enrich
the collection. Each pink or yellow

twisting periwinkle as mathematically
courteous and out of reach as its Latin
tag (Littorina Littorea). Bones,

artifacts, dead languages: the quaint
defences and plaguey, quarantined jokes
of the old days. The guards lock up.
Safely, the museum collects itself.

Rumours of War in the East

On the front page the advertisements for
newly staked land. Details of soil, water,
drainage and the newest roads. On page two
births and marriages and deaths, drawings
of winter's storm damage to property,
and a bridge swept down the creek
in March floods, floating "like a dismasted
tea clipper" in the lake. An explanation
of a new plough, the appointment of a mayor,
a minister and a station master in the nearest
large town. Page three: Congress, the Indian
question, election addresses. A new wind
band is to play for a dance on mid-summer's
eve. Finally, the weddings of European
princes, an announcement of a new novel
in serial form by Charles Dickens,
Imperial cavalries take up position,
the just set sail to administer the peace.
Lancashire cotton exports continue
to astound the Royal Exchanges.

> Here, then, a selection
> of important items
> for storage or display.
> On the wall beside the
> sunlit window-frame
> the librarian tacks up
> a mounted collection
> of arrow-heads ploughed
> up in the nearby fields
> this Spring. On a table
> underneath she rests a
> careful, copperplate
> explanation (written
> after consulting the

school teacher). Later,
they are to be lent to
the County Museum.
Pleased by the warm day
she picks daffodils and
arranges them next to
her work of scholarship.
The readers have left.
She folds the newspaper
and drops it into
its proper rack.

Note

I was in two minds as to whether to name the speaker of each poem. The sequence has never been conceived as a series of dramatic monologues and if there are elements of narrative there is no hidden plot. The poems do not attempt to capture any real accent or to prop themselves up with research. Some of them spring from a conscious verbal frustration, only finding themselves in a deliberate division between passages of prose and verse. I hope there is no tone of lament; it is certainly not intended that they pose as documents.

Some facts of history seemed so attention-seeking that they would immediately burst out of a poem. If facts are part of the background to these poems (for example, that Mr Gladstone sent warships and troops to the island of Skye in 1882 to quell 'riots') they are important precisely because they seem largely to have slipped out of the British memory. Moved and shocked as one might be by such rediscoveries, I can find no single voice to fill in the spaces now. One recognises that as the rifts in memory have been stretched and thinned — particularly by the physical distances of travel — certain questions concerning the subjects which just happen to be forgotten persist. But, even so, these poems can hardly claim to be answers, avoiding the obvious battles as they do.

The discovery of America, a continuing process, effected the dissolution of certain cultures and identities whilst new maps were being unrolled. Europeans watched through the confident, all-excluding lenses of Empire. And the self-evident truths of the new world did not always reach home. Broader views may have become possible in the vulnerable spaces of the West; however, in the old world, small islands proved even easier targets for colonisation and experiment and have continued to echo greater movements of history with forgettable rapidity. Islands, neatly subject to artistic imagination and political whims, were also being discovered at the same time as they were being cleared. The freedoms of landlord, pioneer or tourist betray the strangest of revisionist memories; leaving their cares behind, they leave a lot to be desired.

The facts of exploration and discovery are one thing. The records — pictures, words or photographs — are another. From the time of the earliest voyages to America artists have been taken along. Sometimes the record is 'brought back'. Sometimes it is intended to remain at the point of discovery. Whether of the 'scene' — holiday beach or desolate forest — or a new home or a family group, it celebrates and confirms both distance and identity. In the nineteenth century even those who had died in the mass migrations Westwards were photographed. Some of the grimmer roots of the poems in this sequence about America will be found in the photographs collected in *Wisconsin Death Trip* by Michael Lesy. There is no picture postcard of the Indian Well near the village of Barker, Niagara County, a few hundred yards from Lake Ontario although the local history society has written it up. The photograph referred to in the title poem is by the New York painter and photographer Nancy Shaver.

For contrast, and to see a strange inversion of the process of discovery and recording at work (the Imperial art at home), one might recall the following:

> The grandeur of the scenery was heightened by the fineness of the day, and still more by the idea that a single puff of wind might prove fatal to us, by raising the whole fury of the Western Ocean. At last came two boats, one belonging to the place and ours besides, but both manned by the *savages*. This alarmed us: we thought that our party must be lost or taken and the arms chest was instantly opened; but the boats approaching we found the natives quite pacific, and several came on board — among others their priest, without whom nothing would induce them to venture near us.

This tone did not spring from the natural perils of a voyage to the new world but it seemed natural enough to Lord Brougham in 1799 as he described St Kilda in his *Tour in Western Isles*. The quotation is noted in Derek Cooper's *Road to the Isles* and he also records that, by the twentieth century, the St Kildans were 'laid low by cupidity: in the manner of Red Indians on reservations they even began charging to have their photographs taken'.

Be that as it may, the photographs of a doomed community have all the power and poignancy of words from a dying language. That way of seeing things cannot be repeated. I was privileged recently to see the original photographs taken by Mr Frank Lowe on St Kilda just before that community was resettled on mainland Scotland in 1930. These pictures were stored in his attic, along with the heavy plate cameras he used, in Bolton. He died in 1985, perhaps appropriately, on another expedition in Canada. The interested reader may see some of his pictures reproduced in Tom Steel's *The Life and Death of St Kilda*.

For convenience in the following list, the man who leaves his island is called the 'exile'. From 'Islanders' on the word is hardly relevant.